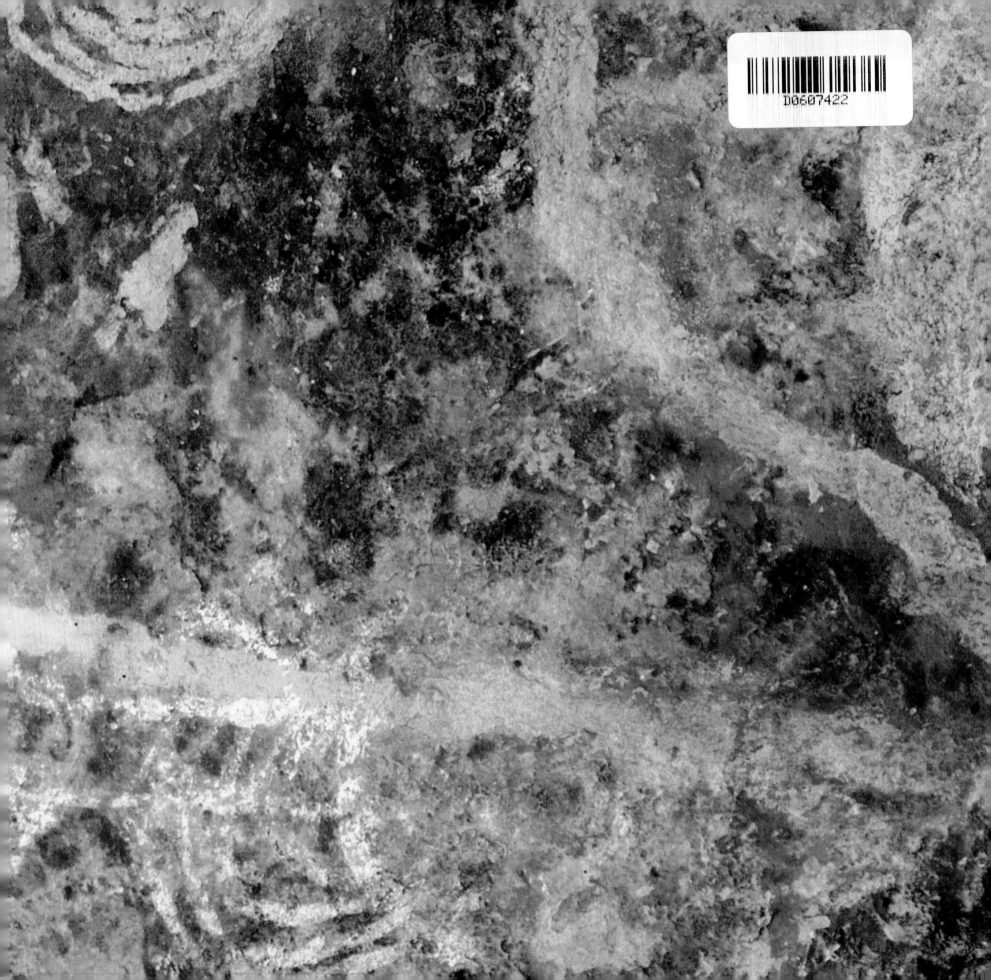

D0607422

MYSTERIOUS PLACES

David L. Fortney

CRESCENT BOOKS

NEW YORK / AVENEL, NEW JERSEY

The Image Bank® is a registered trademark of
The Image Bank, Inc.

Copyright © The Image Bank 1992. All rights reserved.
No part of this publication may be reproduced,
stored in a retrieval system, transmitted
or used in any form or by any means,
electronic, mechanical, photocopying, recording
or otherwise without the prior permission
of the copyright holder.

This 1992 edition published by CRESCENT BOOKS
distributed by Outlet Book Company, Inc.,
a Random House Company,
225 Park Avenue South, New York, New York 10003

ISBN 0-517-06740-4

Printed and bound in Spain

Producer: Solomon M. Skolnick
Writer: David L. Fortney
Designer: Ann-Louise Lipman
Editor: Joan E. Ratajack
Production: Valerie Zars
Photo Researcher: Edward Douglas
Assistant Photo Researcher: Robert V. Hale
Editorial Assistant: Carol Raguso

Title page: **Taking advantage of the cooler hours of evening, a caravan of camels wends its way past the landmark pyramids of Giza that have kept generations of desert travelers company on the perilous, lonely trips across the sandy sea. The pyramids, which dwarf man and beast in age as well as size, had towered over the desert for 2,000 years before camels set foot in the sand.**

DEP. LEG. B-44.001-91

TABLE OF CONTENTS

What makes a place mysterious? Usually, it's a combination of things. Sometimes it's awesome physical evidence of ancient aspirations and superhuman feats—pyramids soaring like skyscrapers against the backdrop of the Nile, giant stone faces standing guard by the sea, massive hidden cities rising up from the jungle. Frequently, it's a puzzle. Why would people etch figures in the earth so huge that no one on the ground can see them in their entirety? How did they move and stack enormous stones without large pack animals, wheels, or block and tackle?

There's magic in mystery, and certain sites have a haunting aura: Stonehenge by moonlight, the Sphinx basking in sun. Add some history, mix in a few legends, and the line between fact and fancy begins to blur. Did the Lost City of Atlantis really exist? What about King Solomon's Mines? Step back in time and examine those mist-covered sites and magnificent monuments where ancient people speak out from the past in ways that we only partly understand today.

Near the south shores of England, villagers of Cerne Abbas and a pagan giant outlined in chalk have been looking out for each other over several centuries. The "Cerne Giant" is a 180-foot-long figure of a naked man holding a club, a god of fertility and the hunt that the Celts scraped on a hilltop 2,000 years ago.

The artists created the outline by cutting away the sod and exposing the white chalk underneath. To keep the lines trim and clear against the surrounding canvas of green and brown, the villagers scour the outline every seven years—showing a respect for primitive art and tolerance for pagan images that early Christians generally discouraged.

Ironically, while this pagan image endured, many English churches were destroyed during the sixteenth century when King Henry VIII declared himself head of the Church of England and issued an edict abolishing all monasteries. Such was the fate of the old medieval church built on Glastonbury Tor, an isolated hill 520 feet high overlooking the Somerset village of Glastonbury.

All that's still standing is an ancient church tower, but it looms over the hill like a lightning rod for legends. According to the medieval story, the Holy Grail, from which Christ drank at the Last Supper and which Joseph of Arimathea used to catch some of the blood Christ shed at the Crucifixion, was brought by Joseph to Britain. Centuries later, King Arthur's quest to find the religious relic led to so many of his legendary adventures. Excavations show the Glastonbury hill was used for burials and in religious ceremonies, either pagan or Christian.

Some people believe both King Arthur's grave and the Holy Grail can be found there.

Several miles east of Glastonbury Tor are two mysterious ringed circles of mammoth standing stones that make the Cerne Giant seem young by comparison. Erected some 4,000 years ago, Stonehenge and the Avebury henge are the oldest, most awesome monuments to paganism still standing in England. Radiocarbon dating techniques indicate that work on Stonehenge began about 2700 B.C.—even before Egypt's famous pyramids.

No one knows who built them, how, or why. Both Stonehenge and the Avebury monument consist of circular, banked ditches, outlined with a ring of awesome megaliths that rise to a height of 13 feet and weigh up to 50 tons apiece—massive stones spanned, at Stonehenge, with horizontal slabs. Most of the colossal blue stones are believed to have come from mountain slopes more than 180 miles away. Moved on sleds and rafts, they were then apparently hoisted into place with rope, timbers, and levers.

While the magnificent monuments were probably built by early Britons for religious rites, archaeologists have noted their careful orientation to the sun. Whoever erected Stonehenge laid it out so that the sun rises over its Heel Stone on June 21, the longest day of the year. Was Stonehenge built as a royal palace or as a temple for sun worship? Or was it an observatory of the heavens for an agrarian people who needed to forecast seasons for planting and harvest? Whyever it was built, Stonehenge is undoubtedly Europe's most famous megalithic monument.

The Avebury henge, or circle, just 18 miles to the northeast, is the largest stone ring in the world. Some 1,200 feet in diameter, its perimeter includes two stone circles—each one bigger than Stonehenge—and part of a village that's sprung up there over the past 300 years.

Along with the standing stones and stacked monuments that jut up from the plains and grassy landscapes of England, there are some mysterious sites that lie half buried under Ireland's emerald sod. Probably most spectacular and curious is the massive stone burial mound built over an underground tomb alongside the River Boyne at Newgrange.

Not only does the site resemble what must have been a truly magnificent underground cathedral for its day, but its construction also displays a sophisticated level of mathematical insight that indicates the structure may have been used to chart the heavens. Whatever the reason for its creation, the mound was clearly the handiwork of a people whose way of life had advanced beyond mere survival levels.

The mound itself is 280 feet in diameter and, in places, up to 44 feet high. Covered for the most part with turf, it stands over a funeral chamber that can be entered through a passageway about five feet tall and lined with large stone slabs. So precisely is the 62-foot-long entrance aligned that sunlight sweeps down the passage and lights up the tomb just once a year—at dawn on the day of the winter solstice.

Some 3,500 years ago, prehistoric people propped up a mammoth circle of stones on one of Scotland's Outer Hebrides islands—a feat that rivals Stonehenge in terms of prehistoric achievement. The standing stones of Callanish appeared on the Isle of Lewis more than six centuries before Solomon even started building his temple in Jerusalem.

Like other circles of megaliths, the stones at Callanish probably served as religious meeting places and community centers for prehistoric people from the surrounding countryside. No one knows whether they were built to honor ancient gods or monitor the planets and seasons, but most contained key stones aligned to the sun, moon, and stars, and megaliths arranged in lines, circles, and other geometric patterns.

Among the more spectacular configurations on the European continent is a giant grid of some 3,000 stones that covers the countryside at Carnac, France. Frozen between the remnants of two prehistoric stone rings, these megaliths stand at attention in parallel lines nearly half a mile long. Like soldiers in column, they are ranked in order of descending height, dropping in size from 20 feet tall in the front ranks to about two feet tall in the rear.

For lack of any convincing explanation of their presence, myths and offbeat theories rush in to fill the void. One local legend claims the stones are the remains of a Roman legion that was pursuing a saint. When he turned to face them and made the sign of the cross, they turned to stone.

Probably the most mysterious place that people have selected to display their art is on the walls of caves—dark, dangerous, damp caverns that not only put the artists in peril but also conceal their work from the light of day. While impressive cave drawings have been found in Norway, Italy, and a ring of North Sea neighbors, by far the best preserved are those in the caves of Lascaux in southern France. There, prehistoric galleries on underground walls display 600 paintings, more than 1,500 engravings, and assorted patterns made up of weird dots and geometric figures that reflect the visions of artists who lived

17,000 years ago. Some of the Lascaux paintings incorporate contours of the cave walls into the art itself, creating effects that are almost three dimensional. Thus, a hole in the rock glares back as the eye of a bison, stalagmites turn into legs, nicks become wounds, and walls bulge outward as powerful shoulders.

On the small Mediterranean island of Malta, archaeological discoveries unearthed in recent years hint that early European civilizations may not have had to import as many ideas from more advanced cultures as scholars once thought.

Radiocarbon dating shows that the enigmatic temples and tombs in Malta are probably the oldest stone buildings still standing in the world. This notion contradicts long-held theories that Egypt and Mesopotamia built the earliest such structures, then gradually passed along their knowledge to the "barbarian fringe" in Europe. Until recent years, most scholars believed that the spiral decorations on many of the temples originated with the Mycenaeans in Greece about 1600 B.C., but the radiocarbon testing shows that construction on the Maltese buildings actually began about 3100 B.C.—long before the arrival of Mycenaean ideas.

Greece does, however, provide us with a variety of locales that continue to resonate with mystery. What setting could be more mystical than Delphi, seat of the most important temple in ancient Greece and home to the all-seeing oracle of the god Apollo? It was here, after all, that people came from throughout the country to consult the Pythia, one of the powerful priestesses through whom Apollo supposedly predicted the future.

The Greeks believed that Delphi, which perched on the steep lower slope of Mount Parnassus, was the center of the earth. According to legend, Zeus, the supreme being, released two eagles—one from the east, the other from the west—directing them to meet at the middle of the globe. The spot where they met at Delphi is marked by a stone in the temple.

Elsewhere in Greece, stones used to fortify the citadel walls of Mycenae are so large that later generations thought they had been built by giants. And some of the characters linked to the city are also larger than life, for this is the home of Agamemnon, the king who sacked the legendary city of Troy. Mycenae was the city that the ancient poet Homer called "Golden," a description that archaeologist Heinrich Schliemann took seriously enough in 1874 to open the now-famous Shaft Graves—an excavation that unearthed an incredible treasure of gold artifacts. Along with the circles of graves and shaft tombs found within the walls of the citadel are the ruins of huge palaces built around great central halls known as megarons.

Off the coast of Greece is the Mediterranean island of Crete, which may still hold clues to the legend of the lost city of Atlantis. The Minoans on Crete had developed a culture beyond that of their neighbors. Not only did they use flush toilets and piped water while others had only wells, they provided their fancier homes with forerunners to air conditioning—devices that let in fresh air and light. The women also had far greater rights than their contemporaries elsewhere.

So here was a brilliant civilization that flourished for 500 years, then suddenly disappeared in the mid-fifteenth century B.C. at the peak of its strength. Most scholars place the blame for the civilization's demise on a spectacular volcanic eruption that occurred in 1470 B.C. on the island of Santorini, 70 miles to the north. So powerful was the explosion that it created tidal waves 300 feet high that crashed into Crete at speeds estimated at 220 miles per hour, and probably brought its Golden Age to an end in a single day.

Crete's capital then was the prosperous city of Knossos, where innovative architects and far-seeing town planners had created an environment similar to that described by Plato, the Greek philosopher who wrote about Atlantis. Could this have been his lost utopia?

The vast continent that borders the Mediterranean to the south is home to pyramids as tall as skyscrapers, swirling desert sands that bury their secrets for centuries, and massive stone ruins that rise unexpectedly from jungle hills. Africa probably embraces a broader range of humanity's ageless mysteries than anywhere else on earth, but no ancient monuments are more awesome than the great pyramids that dominate the Nile Valley skyline near Giza in Egypt. This human-built trio of mountains is the oldest of the classical Seven Wonders of the World—and the only one still standing. Nearly all scholars agree that the pyramids were designed to serve as eternal monuments and everlasting sanctuaries for the vain "god-kings" who reigned in that era. Among the first things a pharaoh would do when he came to power was to start designing the pyramid that would be his tomb. Each seemed to want to outdo his predecessor.

Pressed to satisfy such enormous egos, the Egyptian work force honed their organizational, architectural, and engineering skills to the point where they could produce majestic structures on a scale that amazes us today. Moreover, they did it without draft animals, iron tools, or knowledge of the wheel. And they did it with a precision and craftsmanship that boggles the mind.

The pyramid built for Khufu at Giza, for instance, contains some 2.3 million stone blocks, most of them weighing about three tons apiece, with some tipping the scales at 15 tons. More than 40 stories tall with four sides that are each twice the length of a football field, this grandest of pyramids is the largest stone structure in the world.

The first pyramid built—one of the oldest stone monuments known—is the famous Step Pyramid at Saqqara, which went up during the reign of King Zoser shortly before 2600 B.C. Layered in six stepped-back levels, the 200-foot-tall tomb contains not only Zoser's burial chamber, but an entire complex complete with underground living quarters that duplicated his earthly palace, including false doors and windows, and about 40,000 stone vessels for use in the afterworld.

Largest and most widely known of Egypt's temples are the towering structures at Karnak on the east bank of the Nile, a complex that includes the great sacred temple of the state god Amon-Re. Rebuilt and altered by numerous pharaohs over more than 2,000 years, it's been called a great historical document in stone, because it records the ups and downs of so much of Egypt's history. The complex grew to include an area 400 yards wide by 500 yards long, bristling with a forest of columns.

Among the mysteries that Egypt shares with its neighbors is the awesome Sahara, the world's largest desert. Long feared as a hostile, desolate environment, the Sahara once flourished as a fertile land where rain fell, streams flowed, cattle grazed, and residents harvested grain.

The most convincing record of ancient life in the Sahara comes from the vivid works of prehistoric art found on cave walls and rocks in Algeria, especially at Tassili N' Ajjer. There, in thousands of paintings and engravings that make up one of the world's finest museums of primitive art, a succession of people left their marks between 6000 and 1000 B.C.

Scenes of everyday life show men hunting elephants, tending herds, and fighting each other, while women dance or do their hair. Animals range from sheep and cattle to deer, giraffes, and hippos, indicating that thick grassland and water were plentiful at one time. The absence of camels from older pictures has led historians to divide desert history into two periods, that which occurred before the introduction of the camel and that which followed. Buffalo, on the other hand, appeared in the early drawings but not in the art produced in later centuries.

What killed the Sahara? Scientists can only guess, but one theory is that weather patterns changed after 3500 B.C., thinning out the monsoon rains that swept in from the south. With water evaporating faster than it fell under the scorching African sun, lakes dried up, plants withered, and animals moved on or died.

But fertile land isn't the only treasure that's been misplaced in this continent's misty past. In desert and jungle, adventurers have been looking for legendary wealth left behind in the ruins of ancient cities. In southeast Africa, for instance, European explorers were seeking King Solomon's fabled gold mines when, in 1871, they discovered Great Zimbabwe, the mighty trading center of a forgotten civilization and the heart of a rich, powerful, African empire that thrived from A.D. 1100 to 1450, then disappeared.

It's easy to see how the explorers were misled. Not only was the sophisticated stone architecture a far cry from the simple mud huts found in the surrounding bush, but the ancient city lay in the same general area where Arab traders had long maintained that Solomon's wealth originated.

The city sprawls over a hill, 60 acres of ruins spilling down from an acropolis to a fortresslike enclosure about the size of a football field. All of the structures are made of gray granite blocks, fitted together with great skill and no mortar except for clay and gravel. The enclosure walls are built like a fort—30 feet high and, at their narrowest, four feet thick—but they lack defensive openings and steps for guards to climb. The best guess is that the enclosure was the residence of a ruler who valued his privacy. Even more mysterious is the conical tower within the enclosure walls—what secrets does it hide? Once thought to store gold, it's now known to be solid stone. Perhaps it was a watchtower, or a religious monument.

Like Great Zimbabwe, the splendid, red city of Petra, Jordan, remained hidden from the eyes of outsiders for many centuries. The ancient city has perched on a mountainside terrace far above the desert for about 2,300 years. Approachable only by foot or on horseback, it lies at the top of a mile-long path that winds its way up Petra Mountain, narrowing in places to only three feet wide.

Its inaccessibility made the site attractive to the nomadic Nabataeans, an Arab tribe of caravan traders who settled there about 312 B.C. Not only would Petra be relatively easy to defend, they probably reasoned, but it also stood at the crossroads of lucrative caravan routes. So they chipped and hammered their city into the side of the mountain, embellishing it as they prospered with hundreds of ornate temples, polished tombs, and houses that spilled over onto nearby hillsides.

The city flourished for seven centuries, first as the Nabataean capital and later as an outpost of the Roman Empire. Then sea lanes replaced the camel caravans, commerce dried up, and Petra slipped into obscurity for more than 1,000 years, visited only by local Bedouins until it too was discovered by Europeans in the 1800s.

Unlike easily defensible Petra, Troy is famous for the long siege it withstood until, supposedly, Greek soldiers hidden inside a wooden horse sneaked into the city, opened its gates to their army, and brought the 10-year struggle to a close.

This legend endured primarily because of the *Iliad,* the epic written by the Greek poet Homer about 800 B.C., some four centuries after the Trojan War took place. For centuries the yarn about King Priam's fall intrigued scholars, but most dismissed it as fiction. Then, in 1870, an amateur German archaeologist began a dig in northwestern Turkey at a hill between two streams Homer had described. Not only did he find a lost city, but he also unearthed the fabulous "Treasure of Priam" and gave credibility to Homer's tale.

Along the southwestern coast of Turkey, combative Lycian warriors buried their dead in magnificent rock tombs carved into the cliffs. It was these Lycian villages that Homer described as home to the Cyclopes, the mythological man-eating giants that had one eye in the middle of their foreheads.

While no proof has been found that this legend is fact, the Lycians did leave behind a mysterious network of elaborate tombs carved into rock—virtual cities of the dead similar to the graveyards found at Petra. Some tombs in the cliffs had temple-style facades, while others built on tall platforms took the form of miniature stone houses. Temples or tombs? They look like a combination of both.

No one knows who built them or why, but the labyrinth of caves and underground cities that honeycomb the landscape of Cappadocia in Turkey are a paranoid ruler's dream. Six cities, each capable of accommodating thousands of inhabitants, have been discovered so far. Connected by a network of tunnels up to six miles long, they all have underground water supplies, hundreds of hidden airshaft openings, and secret entrances scattered throughout the rugged mountain terrain.

It's doubtful that anyone lived there continuously, but the cities were probably meant for use in times of trouble by the local inhabitants who lived in tuff formations, their homes carved out of pillars of volcanic rock. With passages just narrow enough to pass one person at a time, they would be almost impossible to storm, and the walls have slots through which defenders could thrust spears.

In western Turkey, giant sculptures of the heads of gods and kings command a view of the heavens near the peak of a mountain called Nemrut Dagi. The enormous heads, toppled from 30-foot-tall statues by earthquakes, stand among ruins of a spectacular shrine to King Antiochus I, who ruled the area in the first century B.C. Ruler of a small but rich state called Commagene, Antiochus spent much of his time and his kingdom's wealth creating monuments to his self-glorification. Along with a huge statue of himself, he built statues of both Greek and Persian gods, reflecting the dual royal lineage he claimed from both cultures. The statues combine similar gods from both religions into hybrid figures, most of them shown seated.

Another great builder, King Darius of Persia, began building a royal palace at Persepolis about 500 B.C. in what is now southwestern Iran. A great leader known for his organizational abilities and diplomacy, he set out to make Persepolis a monument to Persian art and a magnet for wealth.

The project took more than 60 years to complete, continuing through the reigns of the two kings succeeding Darius. Grand as it was, the site usually housed its royal owners for only a few days each spring when they celebrated the new year. However, as a ceremonial capital, Persepolis provided a setting in which regional delegates would compete through the sheer magnificence of their gifts. Unfortunately, rebellions and war with Greece chipped away at the Persian empire until 330 B.C., when Alexander the Great burned Persepolis to the ground.

Modern Iraq is home to the ruins of Babylon. Among the cities that flourished in Mesopotamia 5,000 years ago, Babylon was the grandest—a place of material splendor and moral decadence. Surrounded by an outer wall 10 miles around, the city included a splendid palace and a 295-foot-tall ziggurat—a pyramid-shaped structure called the Tower of Babel.

Built of bricks, the ziggurat consisted of a series of platforms stacked in order of diminishing size. On top was a temple in which deities were believed to step on their way to earth. Many cities had ziggurats, but none was as tall as Babylon's—a point not lost on writers of the Old Testament, who told the story of how Noah's descendants arrogantly set out to build a tower tall enough to reach heaven.

Babylon is also famous for King Nebuchadnezzar's legacy as the greatest builder of ancient times. Among his most magnificent projects was the mysterious Hanging Gardens, one of the classical Seven Wonders of the World. Shaped like a green pyramid of terraces covered with trees and a paradise of plants, the garden was supposedly meant to remind Nebuchadnezzar's foreign wife of her mountainous homeland.

Fabulous cities and amazing ancient buildings grace Asia as well as Europe, Africa, and the Middle East. At Sigiriya, Sri Lanka, a 1,500-year-old fortress with a royal palace and about three acres of landscaped grounds crowns the peak of a six-story-tall boulder. The grounds combine Zen-like rock gardens with the geometrical water gardens and pools of the Persian style. Water for the gardens and pools came from a sophisticated hydraulics system that moved water through underground pipes.

While archaeological digs show people had settled in the area as far back as the sixth century B.C., the rock didn't become the site for a fortress until A.D. 477. That's when Buddhist King Kasyapa I, hoping to find an inaccessible refuge from his enemies, selected the granite pillar known as Lion Rock for his stronghold.

Anuradhapura, the ancient capital of Sri Lanka, was built about 500 B.C. It had colossal Buddhist shrines, some of them as tall as Egypt's pyramids, and covered an area about the size of Chicago.

Anuradhapura was the seat of government when Sinhalese King Tissa and his people were converted to Buddhism in the third century B.C. The city became the headquarters of the Sangha Buddhists, who built bell-shaped shrines called dagobas. After suffering from invasions by the Tamils during the eighth century after Christ, the people fled to another city, abandoning Anuradhapura to the jungle until the British unearthed it in the middle of the nineteenth century.

The city to which the Anuradhapurans fled was Polonnaruwa, which was to become the next capital of the island. Some four centuries later, Parakramabahu the Great expanded the city into a fortress, complete with palace, baths, parks, pleasure gardens, and a number of holy places. Unfortunately, his public works projects strained his kingdom's economy. Succeeding rulers, faced with more invaders, moved on to new capital cities farther south.

After Buddhism originated in India during the sixth century B.C., it spread rapidly throughout much of Asia, blending many of its characteristic art forms with those in regions where it took root. Today, the remains of Buddhist temples and statues still pepper the landscapes in those parts of Asia where Buddha's followers left a religious legacy rich in art.

The Indonesian island of Java is home to impressive monuments to both the Buddhist and Hindu faiths. The Shaiva Temple at Candi Prambanan is the finest example of Hindi architecture on Java—a complex with six temples in an inner courtyard surrounded by four rows of 224 chapels. The main shrine holds a reconstructed statue of Shiva, the Hindu god of destruction and regeneration, which was built in the eighth or ninth century after Christ.

Java's most magnificent—and mysterious—architectural monument is the mountain of faith the ancient Buddhists built at Borobudur. Constructed in the eighth century, the complex includes a nine-level building whose stone terraces circle a lava-covered hill. The building's top levels are the foundation for 72 bell-shaped dagobas, also called stupas, which all contain statues of Buddha. The lower floors house more than 1,300 sculpted panels depicting scenes from Buddha's life. Fully 504 carved shrines of seated Buddhas decorate the temple's terraces.

Buddhism also left its impact on the landscape of China. Early Buddhist missionaries arrived in the first century after Christ, leaving religious relics in small caves along the trade route from India. But it wasn't until the fifth century, after Buddhism had become widespread, that most of the huge carved statues that can be seen there today made their appearance. One of the most striking is the enormous "Leshan Giant," the 21-story-tall statue of Buddha carved into the side of a rock at Leshan in central China.

A sacred site of a different kind appears on the continent of Australia. Eleven stories tall and nearly six miles in circumference, Ayers Rock, a mammoth sandstone landmark, towers over the surrounding flatlands of central Australia like a glowing red monument to the past. As the world's largest monolith and one of its natural wonders, Ayers Rock is a setting fit for ancient gods.

Weather has carved numerous caves at the base of the rock, where, thousands of years ago, Aboriginal artists painted frescoes on the walls. Although some of the art may have satisfied an aesthetic urge, much of it probably played a symbolic or magic role in such rituals and ceremonies as increasing the supply of food or punishing enemies.

Styles of Aboriginal art vary from one part of the country to the next, but three predominate: X-ray painting, which depicts animals from the inside and out, showing their internal organs as well as their exterior shapes; "Mimi" art that consists of tiny, red stick figures, supposedly drawn by tiny fairies that live in cracks between the rocks; and on a larger scale, the Wandjina figures, painted on cave walls in

northwestern Australia, that are up to 14 feet long—spooky white creatures with halos, long-lashed eyes, and black, sausage-shaped snouts.

According to Aborigine legend, the artists who decorated cave walls were ancestral spirits from the "Dreamtime," when the great spirit Baiamee came to earth and created human beings and animals. Some of the mythical artists are even supposed to have painted themselves into their drawings.

The aboriginal people of North America also left their marks on the land. Great earthen mounds topped with flat platforms loom eerily above the plains in many parts of the United States, a legacy of the mysterious Mound Builders' culture. One of the more spectacular ceremonial centers is the Etowah Mounds historic site in Georgia, where a trio of huge mounds towers over smaller mounds on a 52-acre site.

The largest of the orange clay mounds, which resembles a pyramid with the top lopped off, stands 63 feet high and forms a platform that covers about half an acre. The flat-topped mounds dominate two public squares in a village encircled by steep ditches and walls made of pointed stakes.

The Etowah people used this riverside site as a center for commerce, festivals, and burial ceremonies conducted by a priest-ruler. While the smaller mounds were used as graveyards, the taller ones may have been reserved for special rituals. From the top of one mound, visitors can watch the sun rise over a notch in the Allatoona mountains at the summer solstice.

Although most native American mounds were used for burials, the Great Serpent Mound in Ohio presents archaeologists with a mystery. Most scholars believe the five-foot high, 30-foot-wide, quarter-mile-long snake was created by the Adenas, an advanced people who lived in that area up to 3,000 years ago.

But the Adenas themselves are the mystery. Their skeletons show they were powerfully built and big—with many men nearly seven feet tall and women in the six-foot range. No one knows where they came from, but the huge funeral mounds they left behind show they believed in honoring their dead on a grand scale. Even so, the Great Serpent and other animal-shaped mounds appear to contain no bodies.

Wyoming's Bighorn Mountains are the site of the Bighorn Wheel, a giant circular pattern of white stones arranged around what appears to be a "hub" with 28 "spokes." Small mounds of rock are piled on the hub and at six points around the perimeter of the circle, which was constructed 600 years ago. Wheels of a similar design, although less elaborate, have been found in the Rockies.

What were they used for? Some anthropologists say they were probably created for religious rituals, since the design resembles the floor plan of a medicine lodge. Others say the wheels served as astronomical observatories to help farmers keep track of the sun at various seasons. But whatever their function, no one knows why they are located only in remote mountain settings.

Contrary to popular folklore, native Americans had developed advanced, sophisticated cultures long before the Europeans stepped foot on their shores. Among the more remarkable are the so-called lost civilizations that built—then mysteriously abandoned—enchanting kingdoms in the cliffside caves of the sunny Southwest.

The most spectacular ruins are at Mesa Verde, Colorado, where the Anasazi civilization developed from scattered groups of pit dwellers into, by the late twelfth century, a culture capable of building stone-and-mortar cities high in the cliffs. Built on the walls of Soda Canyon, these pueblos on rocky mesas and in cliffside caves are an impressive example of prehistoric architecture.

The dwellings form a network of apartmentlike structures designed for communal living. Up to four stories tall, they contained anywhere from 20 to 1,000 rooms built out of rocks and adobe. Residents plastered or whitewashed the interiors of the rooms, sometimes decorating them with paint. Builders stepped back the upper floors so that the roof of a lower unit became an open porch for the residence above it. Ladders were used for travel between floors.

Among other spectacular cliffside caves the Anasazi called home are the pueblos perched in the sandstone cliffs of Canyon de Chelley in northeastern Arizona. This breathtaking site looks over the bed of a winding river and includes a white-plastered building called the White House that stands at the opening of a cave beneath a towering rock ledge.

Arizona is also the site of an outstanding cliff dwelling called Montezuma's Castle. Built in a cavity 70 feet up the face of a cliff, the five-story dwelling is constructed from boulders, limestone chunks, and adobe. A series of ladders links its 19 rooms. The Anasazi who built the pueblo were descendants of the Basket Maker culture who lived in the region thousands of years before the birth of Christ.

Among the cultures that overlapped that of the cliff dwellers were the desert people who occupied much of Utah and parts of Wyoming, Idaho, and Oregon. The most picturesque showcase for their drawings is in Utah, where Newspaper Rock displays mysterious symbols drawn by different generations. Some of the drawings, which have never been deciphered, are believed to be 1,000 years old. Other petroglyphs are scattered throughout the canyon—the legacy of prehistoric artists who chipped and painted their masterpieces on a sandstone canvas.

Other artists outlined the mysterious, giant figures in the rocky soil of a southern California mesa overlooking the town of Blythe—figures so huge that a traveler could walk across them without knowing they are there. The symbolic landscape includes the 92-foot-long figure of a man, a dance ring, and an animal resembling a horse.

Radiocarbon dating techniques show that these masterpieces were created about A.D. 890, which creates yet another mystery. The native horse vanished from the continent about 10,000 years ago, and its successor didn't arrive until 1540, when the Spaniards introduced it to the Americas. How would a ninth-century artist know what a horse looked like?

In Mexico and Central America, the ancient Maya thrived for almost 15 centuries. While Europe was going through its Dark Ages, these people were developing their knowledge of astronomy to the point where their calendars were as accurate as ours are today. They built great ceremonial centers that took centuries to finish, adorning them with art. Then, suddenly, their culture collapsed. The people abandoned the cities, populations declined, and mighty temples disappeared underneath jungle growth. By A.D. 900, the great ceremonial centers had become cities of the dead.

The city that dominated the last two years of the Mayan empire was Chichén Itzá, a city built around two wells fed by underground streams on Mexico's arid Yucatan Peninsula. Residents drank from one well. Children were thrown into the other. Those who survived their morning plunge into the 60-foot-deep hole were hauled out at midday and asked to report what the gods down there had told them.

To the Mayans, Palenque was the place where the sun died, the westernmost outpost of their civilization. It was also the site of one of the most dazzling cities the culture produced—a city with a towering palace overlooking a courtyard and seven miles of temples and pyramids built along a wooded ridge.

Although archaeologists have so far reclaimed only a fraction of the buildings from the jungle, they have located a secret tunnel in the Temple of Inscriptions that led them to the awesome tomb of Pacal, ruler of the city from A.D. 615 to 683. In the eerie silence of the tomb, which had lain undiscovered for 1,300 years, they found the skeletons of six sacrificial victims and the body of Pacal, his face and body covered with green jade jewelry. Carvings on his sarcophagus and surrounding walls portray the Mayan leader's transition from man into god.

The most elaborate pyramid tomb in the New World, Pacal's resting place was eerily similar to those built for the ancient pharaohs of Egypt. All lie under huge pyramids behind entranceways that were carefully disguised; all were covered by a sarcophagus with his likeness; all lay alongside material objects left for his enjoyment in the afterworld.

Clustered together in a forest area near San Agustín, Colombia, is a group of more than 300 fierce-looking stone statues. Ranging in size up to 21 feet tall, they have scary faces and mouths with catlike fangs. Some appear to be holding and eating children. Some scholars speculate that the area, which is near the ruins of some Stone Age tombs and temples, may have been used for some kind of sacrificial ceremony.

The designs on the tombstones differ from others in South America, but the monuments are similar to those on Chile's Easter Island. Archaeologists using carbon-14 dating techniques have determined that the San Agustín monuments were created between the fifth and twelfth centuries after Christ, but the graves date back about 2,000 years.

Of all the symbolic landscapes people have created on this planet, the most spectacular are the Nazca lines of southern Peru—enormous drawings scraped into the floor of the desert.

Figures up to 900 feet long include several drawings of birds, animals, and reptiles. There's also a man with a halo, a whale, a flower, and a huge spider that is so accurately drawn that scientists have been able to identify it as a rare species found only in certain areas of the Amazon jungle. Along with the figures are several geometric designs and countless lines that fan out in all directions—one of them five miles long.

Scientists say they're the work of the Nazca people, a mysterious culture that probably inhabited the site 500 years before and after the birth of Christ. A vanished race, they farmed, buried their dead in a womblike position, and apparently had no written language. But they could draw on a scale and with a precision that no other culture has matched.

The Incas, another ancient South American culture, founded their capital at Cuzco and ruled a domain as vast as the Roman empire from

this Peruvian city. From their mountain empire, the Inca lords known as "Sons of the Sun" had created cities of sparkling fountains, granite shrines, and stairways fitted together out of unmortared stone. They had also accumulated unbelievable treasures of gold and jewels. However, their remote outpost, Machu Picchu, was to be the last refuge of a ravaged people.

The Inca civilization was already old when the conquistadores landed on the coast of Peru in the early 1530s. Led by Francisco Pizarro, the conquistadores sacked the Inca cities, melted down their treasures, enslaved their people, and murdered their leaders in an orgy of greed that virtually wiped out the empire. The Inca nobles who escaped are said to have taken refuge in the hidden city of Machu Picchu, a military garrison shrouded in mist some 7,000 feet high in the Andes. But later, Machu Picchu's residents disappeared into the jungle, leaving behind the remains of an empire with no one to rule.

When the Spaniards reached the ancient city of Tiahuanaco in present-day Bolivia in the 1500s, the ghostly site was already a majestic ruin. Legend says the city was built in a single night by giants who were later destroyed by the sun. Although the statues and stone blocks used in the buildings appear large enough to be the handiwork of giants, scientists say they were the work of normal-sized people who lived as far back as 200 B.C. Archaeologists digging through various strata have determined that Tiahuanaco is the site of five different cities, one built on top of the other.

Giant-sized, too, are the brooding stone figures standing guard on Easter Island off the coast of Chile. Each weighing up to 90 tons, some of these colossal statues stand 32 feet tall. An intimidating crew, they're scattered over the Polynesian island where a Dutch explorer discovered them in 1772. What he found were hundreds of statues mounted on stone platforms and several more lying only partly finished in a quarry of volcanic rock.

Why were they abandoned unfinished? That's just one riddle that continues to puzzle scholars today. Why were they built, and how were they moved? One experiment showed that it took the efforts of 180 men just to budge one statue—and there may have been more than 3,000 statues at one time. For an island whose population numbered fewer than 4,000 natives when it was discovered, the project would have been a staggering task. Who built them and why? Only the giant statues seem to know. And they, like the mysterious cities, forsaken tombs, and fabulous monuments throughout the world, remain silent.

Wielding a club as if he knows how to use it, the Cerne Giant
keeps a watchful eye on his neighbors in the English village of Cerne
Abbas. The image of a Celtic god of fertility, he is said to have the power
to bless his visitors with offspring.

The lonely tower of a crumbled church continues its ancient vigil over
Glastonbury Tor, the site to which medieval legend says Joseph of
Arimathea brought the holy chalice from which Christ
drank at the Last Supper.

The remains of King Arthur supposedly lie near these church ruins at
Glastonbury, where legend says he was buried. Although scholars believe
that King Arthur really did exist, they say his story probably was based on
the life of a sixth-century Celtic warrior who neither searched for the
Holy Grail nor had a group of followers known as the
Knights of the Round Table.

Left: What time could be more fitting to capture the eerie mood of Stonehenge than a moonlit night when the sun has just fled? Probably built by ancient Britons to honor their gods, these mysterious circles apparently doubled as religious temples and heavenly calendars. For centuries, they've been credited with the power to do anything from increasing fertility to destroying enemies. *Above:* Less frightening by day, they stand alone in a broken circle in the middle of an empty plain.

Above: Although 100 of the prehistoric monuments at Avebury still stand, thousands were destroyed to build village homes and streets. One of the most impressive features about the site is the size of its perimeter, which encircles not only half of a village but two stone circles as large as Stonehenge. *Right:* This skeleton found among Avebury's burial sites was probably interred about 3160 B.C.

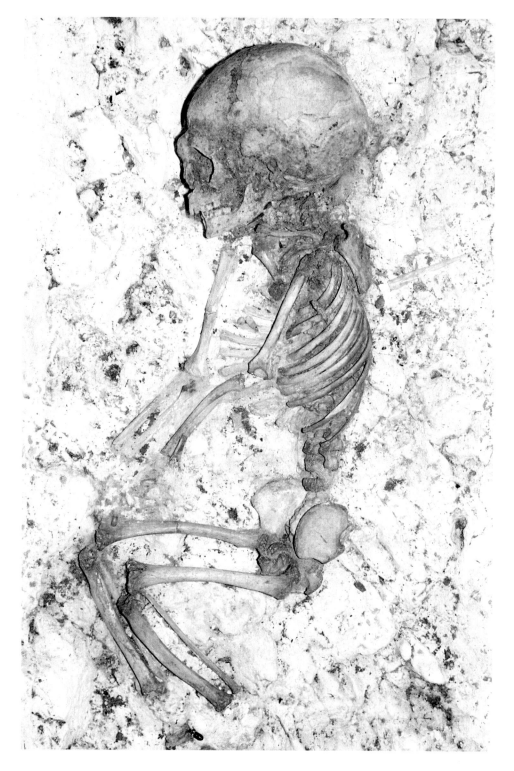

A ring of stone monoliths stands in formation along the shoreline of
the Isle of Lewis in Scotland's Outer Hebrides, preserving a monument
that's weathered the wind and rain of 35 centuries.

From the air, the burial mound at Newgrange looks like a giant, overturned saucer covered with grass, ribbed with rock, and pitted with archaeological digs. Although the mound is huge—almost as broad across as a football field is long—its most interesting secrets lie buried in underground passages.

Why was this awesome earth shrine built? Was it created out of respect for the dead? Or was it meant to serve the living—possibly as some kind of primitive observatory to help farming people chart phases of the moon and seasons of the year? Perhaps, like many other megaliths built by primitive peoples, it was built to fulfill both needs.

There's little room for doubt that the building plan had a heavenly orientation. The entrance to the tomb is laid out so that rays of sunlight penetrate a slit in the roof box, edge their way down the length of the passageway, and finally hit the rear wall of the cruciform chamber. Within moments, the 20-foot-high vault of the burial chamber is flooded with light. Amazingly, this unique phenomenon occurs only at dawn on the morning of winter solstice, the shortest day of the year. Did this coincide with some special religious ceremony? Or did it just serve the more practical function of letting farmers know that winter had turned a corner, that longer days and warmer weather were on the way?

Archaeologists say that the tomb at Newgrange, which is believed to date back to 3000 B.C., was also used as a graveyard for pagan kings. The roof of the funeral chamber itself is a vaulted shell of overlapping stones stacked in horizontal layers. Throughout the tomb and at its entrance, huge stones are designed with cup-and-ring patterns similar to markings found on many megaliths scattered throughout England. No greater tapestry of spirals and other geometric shapes can be found on any other megalithic monuments.

Another unique aspect of Newgrange is its outer ring of standing stones. No other passage-grave tombs, such as those at Dowth or Knowth (also in Ireland), were circled by monoliths. Unlike the stones within the monument, the twelve that remain standing at the site are not covered with designs and show signs of erosion by water, which may mean they originally came from the River Boyne.

Thousands of giant stones ranked by height stand in long lines near Carnac, France, where they've been waiting at attention for thousands of years.

The monoliths of Europe are the oldest in the world, planned and propped up by Neolithic people who had only bone and stone tools and knew nothing of the wheel. These huge standing stones, clustered at scattered sites, loom like ghosts from a misty past.

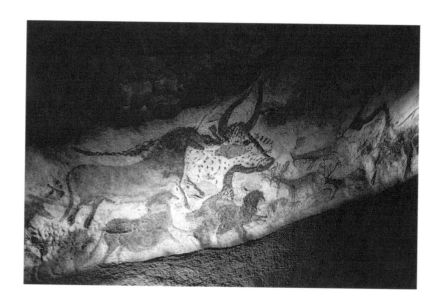

Above: Herds of animals have been stampeding across cave walls at Lascaux, France, for the past 17,000 years. The best preserved of any cave drawings in Europe, the Lascaux paintings lay hidden until they were discovered in 1940 by four teenagers looking for underground passages to an old manor. *Right:* In Lascaux's Hall of Bulls, magnificent creatures up to 120 feet long snort down from walls at heights up to 15 feet above the floor of the cave. Holes in the wall show where pegs once supported scaffolding to help artists reach the higher extremes of their "canvas."

Little is known about the ancient people who carved these petroglyphs into rocks in Norway, but it's certain the Bronze-Age artists were familiar with Viking-style ships.

Petroglyphs cut into cave walls on Levanzo Island near Palermo,
Sicily show an 18-foot-long black panel of lively animal and human
figures. Carbon dating shows that the prehistoric drawings
are almost 30,000 years old.

An ancient temple still standing on Malta shows the enormity of
the limestone slabs that went into the outer walls. Fitted together without
mortar, the walls were topped by stone bricks and cornices.

Malta's temples and tombs are believed to be the oldest such structures still standing anywhere in the world. Their construction dates back to 3100 B.C., long before Egypt's pyramids.

Ancient temple columns glow in the sun at the sacred precinct of Delphi, mythological center of the universe and home of Apollo's most powerful oracle—the shrine from which the Greek god supposedly answered questions about the future. His answers came through the medium of a priestess, who sat in a trance, half hidden by sulfurous fumes, and babbled ambiguous messages that priests would interpret in verse.

Although no records have been found that vouch for the oracle's accuracy, the Greek historian Herodotus claims that King Croesus of Lydia sought its advice before going to war against Persia about 600 B.C. The priestess reportedly told him that he would destroy a great empire by launching such an attack. So he did and she was right—but the empire he destroyed was his own.

The fame of the oracle grew throughout the Greek world and by the sixth century B.C. it was one of the most popular pilgrimage sites, with people coming from far and wide to hear the divinations every month during the spring, summer, and fall. Among those who supposedly consulted the Pythia, or priestess, were Oedipus, Agamemnon, Philip of Macedon, and Alexander the Great, who was told, "My son, none can resist thee."

Not only was Delphi a place of prophecy, but because it attracted so many people, it also became an important meeting place for people from all the Greek city-states. Each city-state had its own treasury at Delphi to which its people would come to make offerings to Apollo. To honor Apollo further, the Pythian games were organized. This event was originally a series of artistic competitions, but later became an athletic contest that was second in importance only to the Olympics.

Excavations show that Delphi has been inhabited continuously since the fourteenth century B.C., but remains of the earliest periods, especially those predating a damaging fire in 546 B.C., are scanty. Centuries of occupiers removed much of the temple treasure, and later the Romans pillaged it frequently. The emperor Nero alone is said to have carried off 500 statues to Rome in A.D. 66. After the Christian emperor Constantine plundered the site, it fell into final decay.

Systematic excavation since 1892 by archaeologists make it possible now to trace the plan of the precinct of Delphi and identify many of the buildings. *Opposite, left:* French archaeologists rebuilt the Athenian Treasury in the early 1900s by fitting together scattered pieces, including two columns of the Doric style used in the Athenian Parthenon. *Right:* Although these three columns were pieced together by archeologists, the Tholos at Delphi once consisted of a large rotunda completely encircled by columns.

These pages: Sprawled across a hilltop in mainland Greece, the prehistoric citadel
of Mycenae is lined with walls of sturdy stone. Excavations in one of the grave circles
in which the royalty had been buried yielded a fabulous treasure of gold and silver
artifacts. By 1300 B.C., the Mycenaeans had expanded their empire throughout
the Aegean world, but some great threat seems to have caused them to
fall back into a defensive posture. A well that had been hollowed into solid rock
at Mycenae indicates that the residents had gone to great lengths to
prepare the citadel for a long siege.

Fancier homes in Crete featured piped-in water and devices used to
funnel outside breezes into the buildings, forerunners of our air-conditioning
systems. Large numbers of terraced roofs and open courts created drainage
problems the Minoans solved by building conduits and clay water pipes,
using drains for both rainwater and sewage.

Large earthenware jars used for storage like this one found in the ruins of a temple at Itaxia once held grain, wine, or oil. Treasures were usually contained in cists, sometimes lined with lead, that were sunk into stone floors.

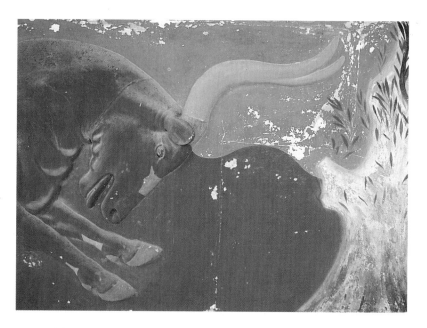

Above: Minoans did little sculpture in the round, except on a small scale using materials like ivory and soft stone that could be easily carved. Much of their art included figures of bulls, which played a role in one perilous ceremony during which young men would apparently somersault over their horns. *Right:* The Minoans built no large temples, using their architectural talents instead to create splendid palaces and sophisticated housing. Their palaces were sprawling complexes with hundreds of rooms built on several stories.

Left: Minoan women, depicted in this wall painting from about 1500 B.C., had rights far greater than any other women of their time. They held influential positions, owned property, and could ask for a divorce. They also controlled their own dowry and, in case of divorce, could reclaim property they had given their husbands during the marriage. *Above:* The temple of Knossos at Crete, the Minoan palace complex, was excavated in the early 1900s by Sir Arthur Evans.

The three great pyramids of Giza have puzzled visitors for centuries. Why were they built on such a massive scale? What gold, mummies, and artifacts do their secret passages hide? Grave robbers, treasure hunters, and archaeologists have undoubtedly removed most of their contents, but plenty of mysteries remain.

The center pyramid was built for Khafre, the pharaoh who supervised the building of the Sphinx. The pyramid in the background housed his father, Khufu (in Greek his name was Cheops), and the smaller one in the front honored the pharaoh Menkure. These Egyptian kings thought of themselves as living gods, who, after they died, would join the other gods, including the most powerful— the sun god Ra. In preparation for their afterlife, they built the pyramids as final dwellings for themselves.

To create these dwellings, not only did millions of blocks of limestone weighing up to 15 tons apiece have to be moved for miles without benefit of pack animals or even the wheel, but many also had to be hoisted hundreds of feet up the steeply sloped sides of skyscraper-sized structures. How did they do it? Probably through a combination of sleds, log rollers, ramps, and the muscle power of thousands of workers.

The engineering marvel began at the quarry, where laborers fitted wooden wedges into slots in the stone, splitting off chunks that were hammered into rough blocks. Eased onto logs, the stones were rolled to barges and floated down the Nile to the construction site, where they were again slid onto logs for rolling. As the pyramid grew, workers built a spiral of ramps around its walls to enable them to hoist the heavy stones to ever-mounting heights. The number of stones used in the building of the pyramids was so great that Napoleon once estimated that they could form a wall around France a foot thick and ten feet high.

But perhaps the most amazing feature of the pyramids is the precision with which they were built. Modern measuring tools show that the foundation of Khufu's pyramid, which covers 13 acres, is so even that there's less than half an inch of difference in height among the four corners.

Although scientists have long known that the pyramids were built as royal
tombs for ancient god-kings, some scientists have wondered if they haven't
doubled as solar monuments, especially since worship of the sun played
such an important part in the religion of the early Egyptians.

Khufu's pyramid, for instance, was nearly perfectly aligned, so its
sides squared almost exactly with the axes of north and south, east and
west. So finely fitted are the blocks that a knife blade cannot be
inserted in the cracks between them.

Preceding page, left: Saqqara is the site of the famous Step Pyramid. Technically not
a pyramid because its sides rise in a series of steps instead of a smooth slope, it
was the first monument in which stones, rather than mud bricks, were used as the basic
building units. *Right:* The temples at Karnak, legendary birthplace of the great
Egyptian sun god, sprawl over an area large enough to cover almost 40 football
fields. *Above:* The site has a virtual forest of pillars and massive columns the
largest of which are the 12 columns in the great Hypostyle Hall.

These pages: Ramses II, Egypt's greatest builder, had the kind of ego you would expect of a pharaoh who called himself king of kings. Boastful accounts of his exploits and courage survive on all major temples of his era, including that at Karnak. His 67-year reign at the beginning of the 13th century, during which he left more monuments to himself than any other self-glorifying Egyptian king, marked the high point of the age of the pharaohs.

Above: The face of an Egyptian child, a 1,500-year-old mummy, stares up from the floor of the Qasr el Ghueita, a Ptolemaic temple built at the oasis in Kharga before 220 B.C. Because early Egyptians believed the dead needed their bodies in the afterlife, they developed embalming techniques that still mystify scientists. *Right:* Rock drawings in the Sahara show humans with animals like the giraffe, which disappeared from the desert thousands of years ago when rain patterns shifted, drying up lakes and driving off most forms of life.

Scientists use these paintings, which number in the thousands on the rock
walls and caves in a mountainous stretch of the desert in Algeria, as
the basis for their theory that the inhospitable Sahara once
flourished with animals and plants.

Some artists have etched their work on the same stone "canvases" used by their predecessors, sometimes superimposing the art of one century over that of another. Together, the paintings and carvings are said to comprise the world's greatest collection of primitive art.

The oldest section of the ancient trading center at Great Zimbabwe is the acropolis, which perches atop a rock ridge about 250 feet uphill from an enclosed temple. Behind the door is a once-secret passage that snakes through the structure's granite block walls.

This conical tower inside the walled temple of Great Zimbabwe has triggered more curiosity than any other ruins found in the ancient city. Treasure hunters and archaeologists have dug around, tunneled under, and removed rocks from the silo-shaped structure— only to learn that it's solid.

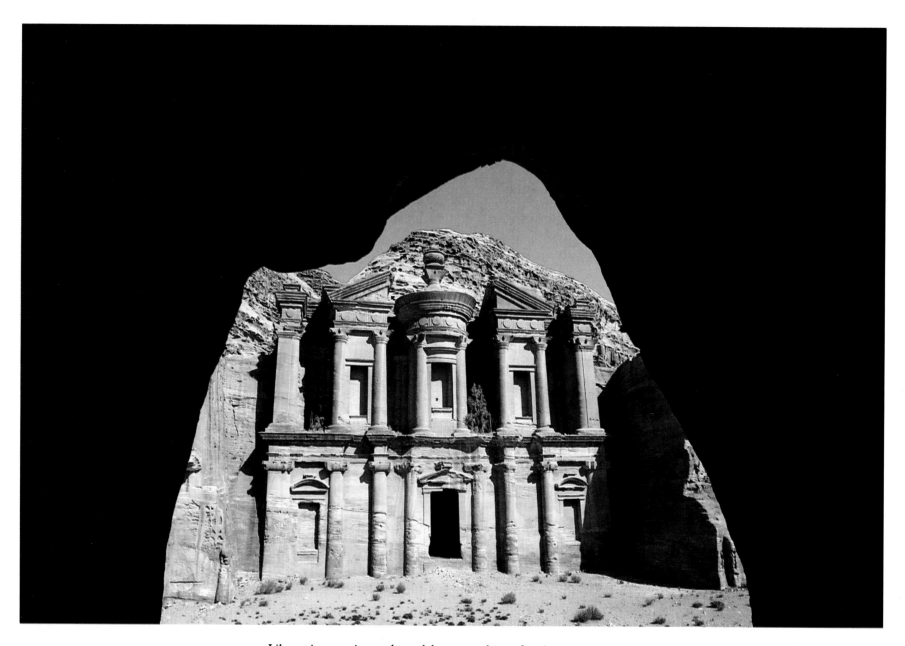

Like a giant movie set, these elaborate sandstone facades put up a good
front for the royal tombs carved into the mountain walls behind them.
Scholars suspect the Nabataeans may have used these cliffside
monuments as temples as well as tombs.

Largest is the 130-foot-tall Pharaoh's Treasure, which was built about A.D. 200 and is rumored to hide a fortune in gold. Along with the ruins of the Nabataeans, the city contains such touches of Roman splendor as an immense hillside theater built to seat 3,000 citizens.

Preceding page, left: Bedouin families still live among the ruins of Petra, dwelling for the most part in homes tucked away in tomb chambers built into the side of the sandstone mountain. *Right:* The Nabataeans had a script similar to Aramaic, the language spoken in Jerusalem during the lifetime of Jesus, but they spoke Arabic. Many of the tombs bear inscriptions in Nabataean or Latin, depending on their occupants. *Above:* Like a shadow from the past, a replica of the Trojan horse looms ominously over the ruins of Troy.

Certain great stories burn in the minds of people and never die. Such is the fate of the story of the Trojan War, retold by the Greek poet Homer in his *Iliad* and *Odyssey*. The epic poems, which were based on an oral tradition, tell the story of the Trojan prince, Paris. According to ancient legend, he judged a beauty contest between three Greek goddesses. As a reward for choosing Aphrodite, he was awarded the love of Helen of Sparta, the most beautiful woman alive. Unfortunately, Helen was already married to King Menelaus, and when she was taken from Greece to Troy, a terrible war ensued, which raged on for ten years. Finally, Athena, the goddess of wisdom, suggested to the Greeks that they build a large wooden horse and hide a few soldiers inside it. The Trojans thought the Greeks had given up the siege and left the horse as a peace offering, so they brought the horse within their walls. That night, under the cover of darkness, the concealed soldiers opened the gates of the city, enabling the remainder of the forces, which had only pretended to leave, to get inside.

Homer's Troy, magnified by the imagination of a poet who wrote about the siege some 400 years after it happened, was much larger and grander than the real site was, but he was very exact in locating his city. The citadel measures only about 150 by 200 yards, a scaled-down version of Homer's glamorous palace that makes the yarn more believable through its vulnerability.

Although its size seems quite small by today's standards, it's probable that the walled city was surrounded by other dwellings made of wood or some other substance that would not have survived the centuries. The houses that do survive were built within the walls on terraces that rose toward the center of the citadel.

The surrounding walls themselves were constructed from limestone blocks set in two levels. The sloping lower level was topped by a vertical stone structure. In one place the foundation goes down 23 feet, and may have supported a lookout tower as tall as 65 feet. The fortifications, which were impregnable to the Greeks until they tricked the Trojans, were unlike any others in the Aegean world.

Above: The Trojans rebuilt their city many times, reinforcing parts of the walls with small stones. *Right:* Actually, there have been nine cities of Troy, all built on the same site. The first settlement went up more than 4,000 years ago, a royal capital fortified with walls. The seventh city superimposed on the site may be the Homeric Troy that was ruled by King Priam.

The hidden cities of Troy lay under the mound of Hissarlik, a hill that rose about
105 feet above the plain three miles from Turkey's northwestern coast. The German
archaeologist who discovered the site was Heinrich Schliemann. His boyhood dream
had been to discover the Troy he had read about in Homer's *Iliad* and *Odyssey*.
Until Schliemann made his find, most scholars considered the Trojan legend
to be fiction based on myth rather than history.

These pages: Ancient Lycians, who lived in a league of
seven cities along the coast of southwest Turkey,
buried many of their dead in cliffside tombs. Hewn
out of solid rock, the elaborate graveyards had facades
that resembled Greek temples. Isolated by rugged
terrain and a fierce reputation, the Lycians kept
for the most part to themselves.

These pages: These tuff formations at Cappadocia in Turkey were the dwellings of a very defense-oriented people. Not only did they carve houses out of these strange pillars of volcanic rock, but they also created miles of impregnable tunnels, passages, and rooms underground.

The head of a giant eagle stands beside the heads of gods and kings that
watch over the kingdom of Commagene from the mountain of Nemrut Dagi
in western Turkey. The mountain's 7,031-foot summit is capped by
a cone-shaped mound built from rocks chipped from ledges on which
the statues' bodies sit. The 30-foot tall statues were
beheaded by earthquakes.

The Persian god Mithras surveys the landscape along with the other Persian
and Greek gods who were worshipped in the kingdom of Commagene.
King Antiochus I, who ruled over the region, claimed to be a
descendant of kings of both Persia and Greece. The statues blend
styles native to both cultures.

These pages: Construction of the ancient city of
Persepolis in present-day Iran began about 500 B.C.
under Darius the Great. Hundreds of columns went into
the construction of a large, ceremonial palace,
especially in the huge audience chambers and the
famous Hall of Columns. Curiously, there were
no temples built in the city.

Preceding pages, left: Figures in carvings at Persepolis, such as these, are usually
flatter than those found in sculpture created by the Greeks. That was done in an effort
to make sure that the sculpture on the walls would not detract from the more
important ceremonies taking place in the foreground. *Right:* Persian sculpture often
combined into a single mythical figure the legs, wings, bodies, and heads of
different animals to symbolize a range of qualities worthy of royalty. *Above:* Only
the skeleton remains of an audience hall that once held 10,000 people and their
annual tribute — gold jewelry, ivory, and a menagerie of animals ranging
from camels, giraffes, and horses, to bulls and honeybees.

Above: Stelae found among the ruins of Babylon show scenes in which heavenly beings walked among the people. The gods supposedly had human features and feelings and involved themselves in worldly affairs. *Right:* Walls and temples were adorned with the likenesses of sacred animals.

Builders used sloping ramps and stairways to break up the monotonous surfaces of the huge ziggurats. Bitumen and reeds were often placed between layers of bricks to strengthen the walls.

Stone doorsteps of palaces and monasteries were usually flanked
by solid balusters and the likenesses of the feet of large animals. The
architectural styles of Sri Lanka strongly resemble those of India.

Terraced gardens and pools of water embroider the landscaping on the top of Sigiriya. A Buddhist king built the fortress on top of a large granite boulder to protect him from his enemies.

These pages: Maidens with golden skin and enticing eyes grace the
Sinhalese frescoes painted along the path through King Kasyapa's 1,500-
year-old gardens. Only 21 of the original 1,500 paintings remain
on the polished walls.

Most remarkable of the archaeological remains found at Anuradhapura are the enormous Buddhist dagobas, the bell-shaped shrines built of sun-dried brick that rival Egypt's pyramids in height. Towering up to 40 stories above the ground, the dagobas are simple architectural forms capped by domes that are bell- or lotus-shaped. A strict ritual guided the positioning of the foundation stones. Materials used included a rubble core, covered with brick and stone and finished with plaster, which was then painted white. The main approach always faced south. The Ruanveli dagoba at Anuradhapura was designed as a giant model of the universe.

Along with its religious architecture, Anuradhapura is home to a famous 2,000-year-old bo tree—an offshoot of the tree along side a tributary of the Ganges River under which Buddha found spiritual enlightenment after fasting for 40 days. The Sinhalese king and people of Anuradhapura were converted to Buddhism in the third century B.C. by Mahendra, a Buddhist monk sent there from India. It was he who brought and planted the bo tree that stands there today.

The Sinhalese Bhikkhus, or monks, belonged to the Theravada sect of Buddhists, who took vows of celibacy and poverty. Living first in caves and later in monasteries, they brought with them a knowledge of sculpture and architecture. The city eventually became headquarters for the Sangha order of Buddhists, who built the vast dagobas. Under Buddhism, an advanced civilization developed, including such projects as some large-scale irrigation works that continue to irrigate crop land today.

Not only was Anuradhapura once the seat of Buddhism in what is present-day Sri Lanka, it was also the seat of government. A magnificent city was conceived by King Dutthagamani and built at this site by his order around the first century B.C. At least nine colossal public buildings were erected, the largest of which was said to have 900 rooms complete with fabulous sculpture and paintings, and silver furnishings.

Left: Among the wealth of splendid statues and engravings of Buddha that dot the Sri Lanka countryside is the 44-foot-long reclining Buddha built into a rock wall at Polonnaruwa. The granite statue is one of many religious monuments ordered built by Parakramabahu the Great. *Above:* A stone statue shows Buddha seated in his traditional meditating posture, with his legs crossed in the lotus position, his hands clasped in his lap.

Both ancient Buddhist and Hindu temples are found in Sri Lanka.
Buddhism was founded about 2500 years ago by a Hindu of noble birth who
achieved enlightenment after fasting for 40 days under a bo tree.

The dagobas, or stupas, that grace the peak of the Buddhists' mountain
of faith at Borobudur are well-preserved examples of the bell-shaped
religious shrines built to honor Buddha 12 centuries ago. This
temple is one of Buddhism's holiest places.

Early Buddhist art in China consisted primarily of small sculptured
figures and paintings left in caves along the trade routes from
India. Most of the bigger statues and rock carvings didn't appear
until the fifth century after Christ, when Buddhism
had become widespread.

The Leshan Giant may look benign in this close-up of its head, but the impact of its 210-foot-tall body as seen from the ground is much more powerful. This statue, carved in the eighth century, is one of the last large stone replicas of Buddha created in China.

Looming over the desert like some giant prehistoric creature, Ayers Rock completely dominates the plains of central Australia. The reddish sandstone landmark, which can be seen from 60 miles away, stands 1,143 feet tall and has a girth of almost six miles. There are no foothills. It juts up abruptly in the middle of the plains, the stark remnant of a much larger mountain range formed some 450 million years ago when the earth's plates shifted. The tremendous pressure buckled horizontal layers of sandstone on the bottom of an ocean, standing them on end in jagged formations.

The sprawling monolith known as Ayers Rock is what remains of those mountains after more than four million years of erosion and sandblasting by wind, rain, and weather. "The rock," which contains no life whatever on its bald surface, is pitted and furrowed with gullies and caves. When it rains, the water snakes down its sides in silvery streams, filling the gullies and spilling over ledges into countless small waterfalls that cascade down the face of the rock–splashing into the open, vanishing, then reappearing with magic rapidity.

So great is the magnificent rock's mass that it even creates some weather of its own. The sandstone absorbs heat during the day, then releases it at night, creating updrafts, downdrafts, and occasional storms that swirl through the plains around it. The cliff walls rise almost vertically, some of them worn smooth, others honeycombed with hollows. The larger caves near the base of the cliffs have been decorated by the Aborigines, who consider the rock a sacred place, a home for their ancestral gods.

Along with its size and shape, another peculiar feature of Ayers Rock is its ability to change color dramatically as the day progresses. From terra cotta to mauve to a fiery red at sunset, the faces of the rock reflect a moodiness that shifts with time and weather. The basic reddish-brown glow of the rock comes from the weathering of large quantities of the mineral feldspar found in the sandstone. Because the upended layers of sandstone vary in hardness, they've eroded at different rates, creating a corduroy pattern along many faces of the rock.

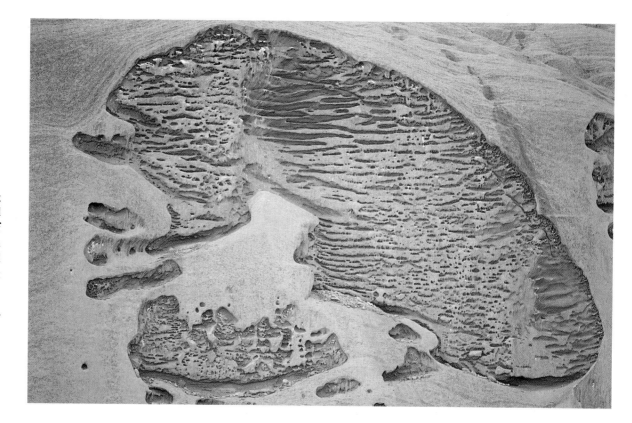

One of the more interesting formations on Ayers Rock is called the Brain, because of the layers of wrinkles that resemble the human brain. Another formation, created by falling debris, is a long, curving arc called the Kangaroo's Tail. *Below:* The Aborigines of western Arnhem Land developed a style of drawing known today as X-ray art. These paintings portray both the exterior forms of creatures and their skeletons and internal organs.

Opposite page, left: "Mimi" line art, found in western Arnhem Land, portrays humans as tiny stick figures about two inches high. The paintings usually show people in a state of motion, crouching, running, hunting, fighting, or throwing spears. *Right:* Even when the figures are shown standing still, they crouch like ballet dancers poised for action. Aborigine folklore says the paintings were done by the Mimis, a thin fairy people who live among the rocks.

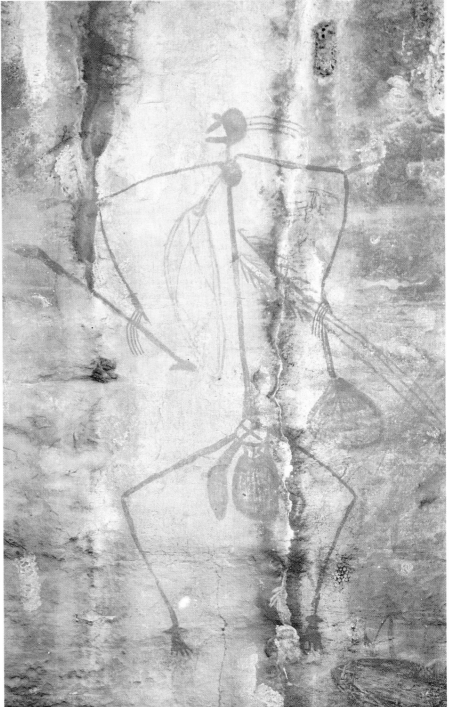

Broad platforms, such as this one in Georgia used for ceremonies, top the truncated pyramids of the Mound Builders, a native American culture that blanketed the southeast. Some of the artificial hills have been around since A.D. 500.

Great Serpent Mound in Ohio, an enigmatic earthwork effigy, is thought to have been created by the Adenas, who built several mounds nearby. Serpents were an important part of the religious beliefs of many peoples, but no one is sure whether the serpent, if it is of a religious nature, represents a benign or malevolent force.

Scholars are still puzzled over the purpose of the Bighorn Medicine
Wheel. Unlike many native American mounds, the elaborately piled stones
don't serve as a burial monument, but instead may have been
a sacred site for ritual dancing.

Left: Abandoned pueblos on a mesa in Colorado's Soda Canyon mark the remains of a 1,300-year-old civilization that advanced from living in pit houses to building communal homes that housed hundreds of families. *Above:* Abandoned after a century of use, the ruins of Mesa Verde are proof that an advanced culture once lived in the area. Most historians believe the Anasazi left their canyon homes when a drought forced them to hunt for a more hospitable environment.

The great Anasazi settlement at Pueblo Bonito in New Mexico's Chaco Canyon once housed more than 1,200 people, who lived in a semicircular structure covering more than three acres.

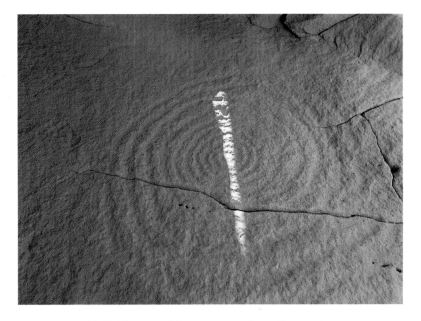

Left: These pueblos represented a halfway point in the development of their housing, a big step up from the pit houses where they first lived, but considerably more vulnerable than the cliffside housing they later constructed. *Above:* A sliver of light at the summer solstice falls on what appears to have been a crude form of calendar found in the ruins of Pueblo Bonito.

Left: Montezuma's Castle stands in a cavity 70 feet up the face of a cliff where it was built some 800 years ago. One of Arizona's most outstanding cliff dwellings, the pueblo has 19 rooms. *Above:* These cliff dwellings at Betatakin, Arizona were home to the Anasazi about 700 years ago.

Pictographs produced by the Anasazi included both simple paintings and figures carved into the surface of rock.

As the Anasazi developed their culture, their art went beyond geometric designs to include stylized birds, human figures, and animals.

Utah's Newspaper Rock is a centuries-old canvas on which generations
of native Americans have scratched figures of animals, humans, and symbols
into the "desert varnish" with which time has covered the stone. No one
has been able to decipher the meanings of the ancient messages.

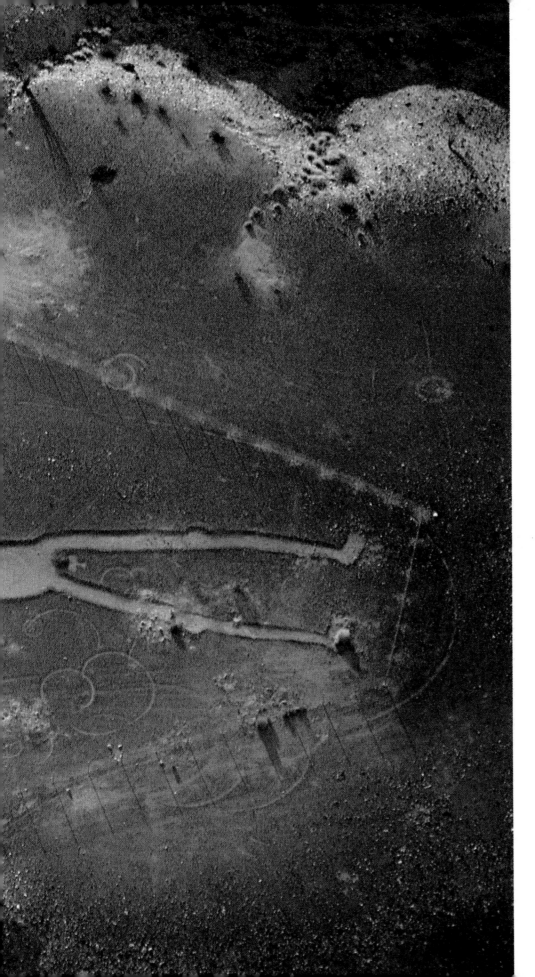

Perhaps the most mysterious place on the North American continent is about 150 miles northeast of San Diego at a site near the banks of the Colorado River. Giant figures of a man, a horse, and what appears to be a dance ring were scraped in the gravel about 1,100 years ago on this mesa overlooking Blythe, California. Why were they drawn so huge that they can be seen in their entirety only from the air? There's not even a nearby hill from which the creators could have seen the results of even part of their work.

Many archaeologists who've studied the figures believe that a tribe of native Americans carved them to express creation myths. However, that's just an educated guess, since no one really knows much about this ancient tribe. Unlike with other pre–European contact civilizations such as the Adenas or the Anazasi, no household artifacts have been uncovered that would allow scientists to compare this culture to others in the region.

However, just by looking at the figures, one can see that the dance ring is reminiscent of the lines carved by the Nazca. The anatomically correct figure of the man, surprisingly, looks very similiar to England's Cerne Giant, and the drawings were even made in the same way—by scraping away at the loose top layer of earth to reveal the hard soil below.

The most amazing and mysterious aspect of the carvings is that they were created about A.D. 890. The horse that was native to the North American continent died out thousands of years before that, and the modern horse was not introduced by the Spaniards until 1540. How could these ancient artists have known what a horse looked like?

Some archeologists and sociologists, called diffusionists, believe that one ancient civilization developed somewhere in the world (some say northern Africa but others differ) and spread around the globe. This would account for similarities in far-flung cultures. However, other scientists, called isolationists, believe that many isolated cultures developed independently and that religious, artistic, or social similarities between distant peoples is merely coincidence. Again, no one knows for sure, but the Blythe figures can be claimed as evidence by both sides.

Most primitive art found in Hawaii is highly stylized, like this petroglyph
of a person falling out of a canoe. Note the strong, simple lines
characteristic of Polynesian drawings.

Ceremonial centers like this temple pyramid stood at the heart of Mayan cities and served as the focal point for all religious activity. The temples were stone pyramids with flat tops, faced with limestone and fronted with a single steep flight of stairs. The priests celebrated their rituals in a masonry temple at the top.

At the base of the Temple of the Warriors in Chichén Itzá stands the Grave of the Thousand Columns, a burial ground for nobles and priests. Both classes lived in luxury, either in palaces or on wealthy estates.

A jaguar's head bares its fangs from the top of the Temple of the Warriors. Above is a figure holding what appears to be a plate—possibly a receptacle for organs removed in sacrificial rites.

Although the Maya had knowledge of the wheel, they did not use it to
help them build impressive structures such as this one. Instead,
wheels were used on toys.

Preceding page, left: The crumbling remains of an observatory at Chichén Itzá still
seem to reach for the sky. Brilliant astronomers and mathematicians, the Maya
priest-rulers used the stars to develop calendars. *Right:* A statue of a deity, perhaps
the god Chac, to whom the Well of Sacrifice was dedicated, lies among the ruins
of the Temple of the Warriors. *Above:* Mayan temples such as this one
at Tulum stand as monuments to the dedication of the artisans who built them.
Every stone was cut without the use of metal tools.

Left: A tower and other ruins of Pacal's palace overlook a courtyard in which teams used to compete in a deadly serious game of ball. To score, players had to put a rubber ball through a stone ring mounted on the wall, using only their legs, hips, and shoulders. The losers were often put to death. *Above:* The Stela of the Sun shows the Mayan style of sculpture, a highly developed art form used to decorate stone, stucco, jade, and wood. Most figures represented in art came from the upper classes.

Huge stone figures stand guard over a clearing in a lush green valley outside San
Augustín, Colombia. No one knows who put them there or what they represent.
Opposite, left: Archaeologists say the mysterious statues are unlike any other stone
figures they have seen in South America. *Right:* An ancient grave site lies near
the San Augustín statues, but experts don't really know any more about it
than they do about the monolithic monsters.

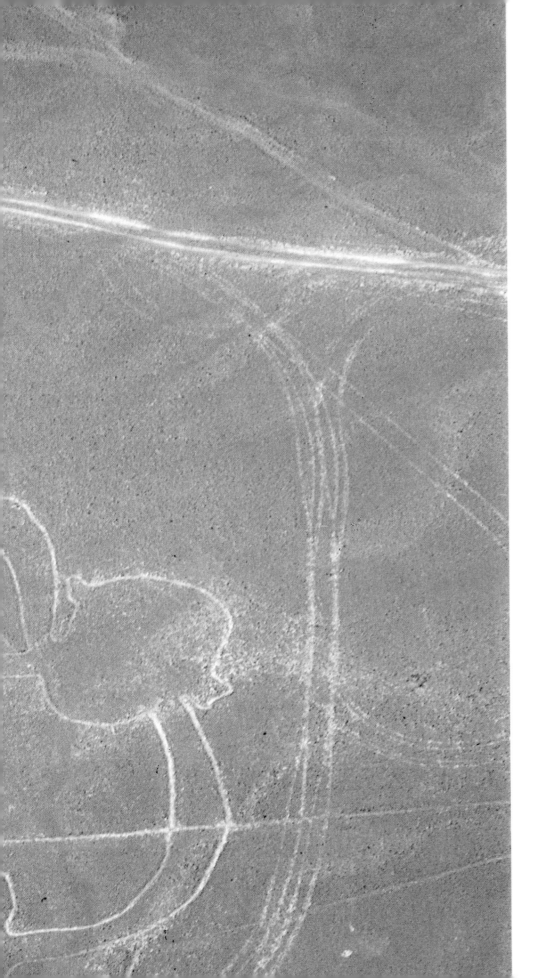

A virtual zoo of animals has sprawled across the desert landscape of southern Peru for the past 20 centuries. Among the carefully crafted drawings are a condor, a hummingbird, a duck, a spider, and a whale. Most figures are depicted by single lines that do not cross.

In addition, there are many geometric patterns—trapezoids, triangles, rectangles, and straight lines—covering an area about 30 miles long and 10 feet wide. To make the delicate lines, some only inches wide, the Nazca scraped away the dark stones to reveal the yellow soil underneath. Parallel rows of pebbles lay alongside the bands of soil.

How do we know the Nazca did it? A vanished race, the Nazca left no written records of their times, but they did leave behind thousands of pieces of pottery using the same style, designs, and figures found in the desert drawings. Carbon dating shows that this pre-Inca culture inhabited the area as far back as 500 B.C.

Archaeologists say the artwork probably occurred in two stages—first the figures whose lines never intersect, and later the long lines and geometric designs that crisscross some of the earlier works. The only reason these drawings have endured all this time, scientists say, is because of the aridity of the climate. Almost no rain has fallen in the desert in the past 100 centuries.

No one really knows what the giant drawings mean. The figures may have been meant to invoke the magical powers of ancient gods, while the lines may have been used in some kind of astronomical calendar to help the Nazca monitor seasons for planting and harvest.

But why were they so big? Why spend so much time and effort on projects that people on the ground can't even see? Some people believe that the ancient tribe had mastered the art of flying with some kind of giant kite or hot air balloon. A few years ago, explorers proved that this could have been done by making a primitive balloon, using only materials that would have been available to the Nazcas. The balloon took them to a height of 600 feet before a sudden burst of wind forced them back to the ground, but they showed that it could have been done. But was it?

The ruins of Machu Picchu sprawl across a site some 7,000 feet high in the Andes of Peru. It was here that Inca rulers are believed to have fled in the sixteenth century to escape slaughter or enslavement at the hands of Spanish conquistadores.

The Incas were noted for their fabulous stonemasonry, such as that used in
creating these lodgings and temples, which were erected without mortar.
The beast of burden used to help carry heavy materials was the llama,
whose long supply trains were essential to Inca builders.

Above: A gridiron of heavy stones marks the foundation of enormous buildings laid out in the city of Tiahuanaco, Bolivia. *Right:* Stones up to 100 tons in weight had to be moved to the site and put in place without the help of large pack animals or the wheel.

Left: Colossal statues stand among the ruins of Tiahuanaco, a site occupied by five layers of cities. No one knows who built the statues, but the Incas were still leaving sacrificial offerings there when the Spaniards landed in the sixteenth century. *Above:* The Incas believed that an ancient tribe of gods built Tiahuanaco, then perished.

Above: Discovered by a Dutch explorer on Easter Sunday, 1722, Easter Island has become famous for its distinctive statues. *Right:* Some of the giants have seen better days, like these found tumbled in a quarry. Apparently abandoned in a hurry, they are only partially complete.

Preceding page, left: When first discovered, most statues stood on stone bases. Later generations of explorers, however, reported that many had been tumbled to the ground, perhaps as a result of a war fought among the inhabitants of nearby islands.
Right: Some of the giant statues display the cylindrical red crowns resembling in shape the hairstyle favored by ancient Polynesian natives. *This page:* A rainbow arches over the statues standing guard on Easter Island.

INDEX OF PHOTOGRAPHY

For rights information about the photographs in this book please contact: The Image Bank, 111 Fifth Avenue, NY, NY 10003. All photographs courtesy of The Image Bank, except where indicated *.